The House of Bindia's Dreams

Written by Nandini Nayar
Illustrated by Ana Sanfelippo

OXFORD
UNIVERSITY PRESS

Words to look out for ...

complicate *VERB*
To complicate something is to make it difficult or awkward.

gain *VERB*
To gain something is to get it when you did not have it before.

involve *VERB*
To be involved in something is to take part in it.

potential *NOUN*
If you have the potential to do something, you are likely to be able to do it in the future.

purpose *NOUN*
the reason why you do something; what something is for

react *VERB*
To react is to act in response to another person or thing.

Chapter 1

When Bindia was small, she thought her house was very special.

It stood in the middle of wide green fields. Deer lived there. Peacocks spread their tails under stormy grey skies.

Amma

Bindia

In those days, Bindia could see all the way to the road. She could even see the shops there.

The bus would roar up, chased by a cloud of dust. In the evening, Baba would get off the bus and walk home.

Baba

The fields had been taken over by houses now. Tall walls kept the deer out. The walls also shut people away from their neighbours.

Noises floated over the walls, though. Bindia heard snatches of songs. She could hear the hiss of a cooker. She heard the boy next door, but could not see him.

Hurrying to school, Bindia dashed past swings and shining bikes. She saw an old man sitting by his front door. She saw the house of the woman she called Plant Lady.

Amma and Baba were too busy to talk to anyone. Bindia was too shy. They lived among people they didn't know.

Chapter 2

One day, Bindia saw a house being painted pink. She saw other houses that were red and blue.

Plant Lady's house had white walls, but it stood in a sea of flowers and leaves.

Bindia's house had dull grey walls. It had never been painted.

"Let's paint our house," Bindia said to Amma and Baba. "I want dark green walls. I want roof tiles as red as Amma's bindi."

"My bindi?" Amma touched the red dot on her forehead.

Bindia's parents didn't <u>react</u> as she'd hoped.

To react is to act in response to another person or thing.

She had thought her idea would make Amma and Baba happy. Instead, they sadly shook their heads. They had no money to paint the house.

This complicated things.

Bindia thought hard. How could she get the house of her dreams?

To complicate something is to make it difficult or awkward.

Chapter 3

The next day, Bindia ran to school as usual. Then she stopped.

She had seen the perfect green for the walls of her house. It was the green of a creeping plant on Plant Lady's wall.

"Do you like my plants?" someone asked.

It was Plant Lady, smiling at her.

"Oh, yes," Bindia said.

Plant Lady gave Bindia some seeds. She told her how and where to plant them.

"Every seed has the potential to grow into a tree," she said.

If you have potential to do something, you are likely to be able to do it in the future.

Bindia saw Plant Lady every day after that.

Plant Lady told her important things like, "Plants need good soil," and, "Water your plants when their soil is dry!"

Bindia tried hard to do what Plant Lady said. Soon, green shoots peeped out of the earth. They gained height each day.

To gain something is to get it when you did not have it before.

Sometimes, though, Bindia's bus was late. Then there was homework to do and Amma to help. She had no time to water her plants.

One hot day, Bindia's class had a project to finish. It was late when Bindia finally went home.

She remembered her plants. What if the sun had burnt them?

When Bindia got home, she was surprised. Drops of water sparkled on the plants' leaves.

After that, the plants were watered whenever Bindia was late. Bindia went to thank Plant Lady.

"It wasn't me," Plant Lady said. She smiled. "You must have a secret helper."

Who could it be?

Chapter 4

The next day, Bindia was home early. She pushed open the gate and stared. Someone was watering the plants.

It was the boy from the house next to Bindia's.

He smiled at Bindia.

"I hope this is all right," his mother said. "He needs friends and a purpose in his day. Could he help you?"

Bindia smiled.

The boy was Amit. He and Bindia watered the plants together. They cheered each time they saw a new leaf.

A purpose is the reason why you do something, or what something is for.

Soon, they were friends.
When the first red flower opened its petals, they danced in joy. Over the weeks, more flowers appeared.

Bindia's smile grew wider. Amit was happy to be involved. It was good to see flowers on the plants. It was even better to have a friend.

To be involved in something is to take part in it.

Then Bindia came home one day and gasped.

Leaves and flowers were scattered on the ground. Plants were bent and broken. Amit reacted by bursting into tears.

"Oh, no!" cried Bindia. "Who could have done this?"

To react is to act in response to another person or thing.

"Squirrels and birds attacked your plants," a deep voice said. "You need someone to watch them." It was the man who spent his days sitting outside his house.

How could Bindia watch her plants? She had school all day.

"I'll watch them for you," the old man said.

His name was Pande-ji.

Chapter 5

Tap-tap-tap, Pande-ji tapped his walking stick. Flap-flap-flap, he rustled his newspaper.

The squirrels darted away. The birds flew off into the sky.

Now Bindia's plants were safe.

The plants soaked up the sunlight and water.

Plant Lady helped the plants grow up the walls. Up and up and up they grew.

People stopped to look at the plants. Neighbours asked about them. Plant Lady, Amit's mother and Pande-ji chatted about them.

Only Amma and Baba didn't notice Bindia's plants. They rushed out to work in the morning. They came home in the dark, too tired to look up.

One day, Pande-ji stopped Baba and Amma. "Look at your house," he said.

Baba looked up at his house for the first time in weeks. He thought he would see dull grey walls. Instead, he saw walls green with fluttering leaves.

When Amma looked up, she saw a bright red rooftop.

"It's as red as my bindi!" she cried.

Everyone talked about what had happened. The plants had made the house of Bindia's dreams.

"No," Bindia smiled. "It's the house of **all** our dreams."

Everyone who had been involved smiled back. They were glad to be among the plants they'd grown and the friends they'd made.

To be involved in something is to take part in it.